Laughable Limericks and
Fun Facts About Animals

Out on a Limerick

Rod Davis

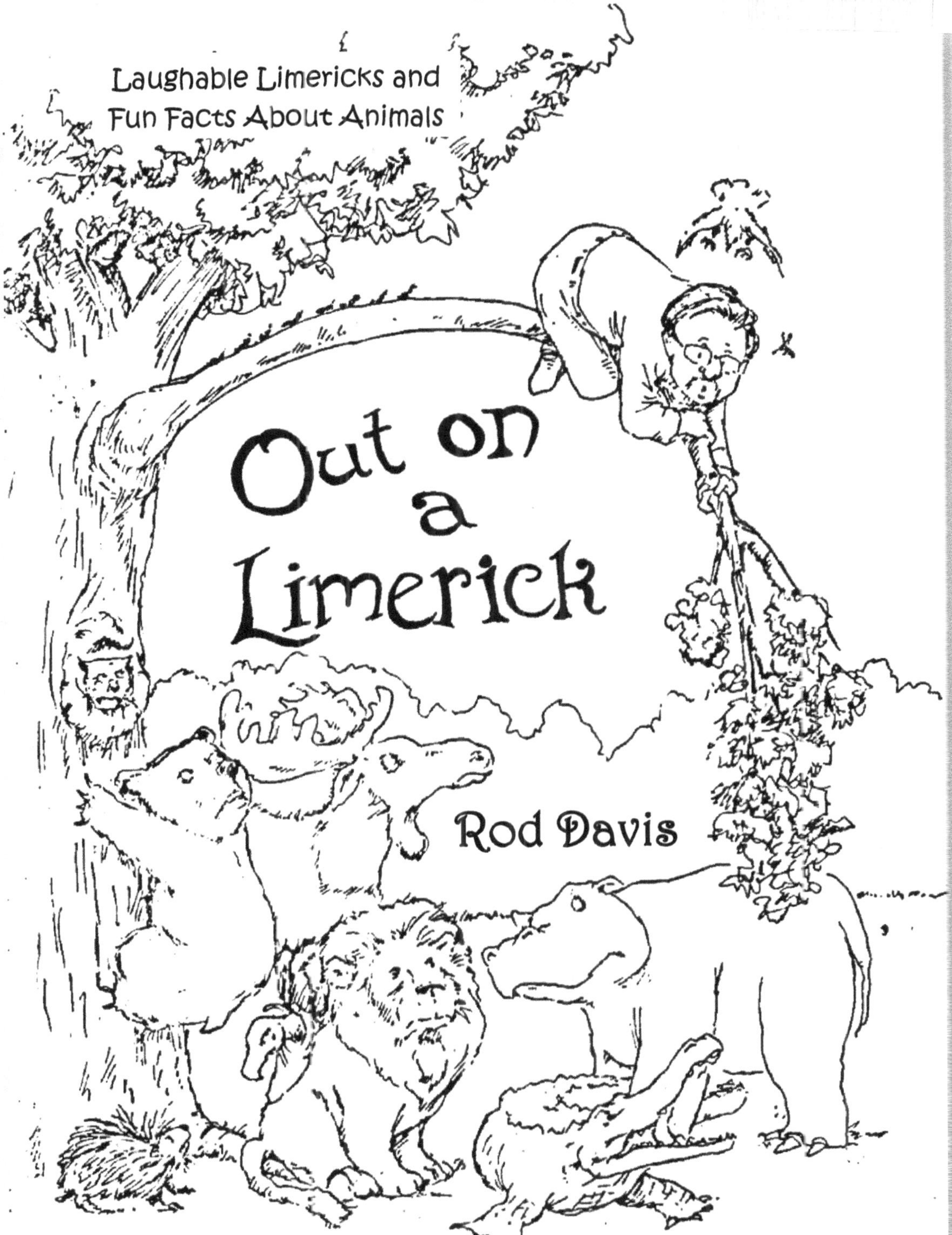

Illustrations by Tom Kerr

Out on a Limerick

Laughable Limericks and

Fun Facts About Animals

Rod Davis

Practically Peerless

Unique Ink Press
18030 Brookhurst St #316
Fountain Valley, CA 92708

Paperback Edition
Copyright © 2017 Rodney G. Davis
All Rights Reserved

Complete International Standard Book Number:
978-0-9847100-5-8
ISBN/SKU: 0-9847100-5-1

No part of this book may be reproduced in any form, stored in a retrieval system, or transmitted in any form or by any means—electronical, mechanical, photocopying, recording, scanning, or otherwise—without the written permission of the publisher.

Unique Ink Press
Practically Peerless

Unique Ink Press
18030 Brookhurst St #316
Fountain Valley, CA 92708

www.uniqueinkpress.com

Dedication:

To a person who called me up about ten years after we first discussed collaborating on this book. He told me these limericks were too good to leave filed away. I hope he was right.

To Tom Kerr

Into this book you truly did dive.
You made these animals come alive.
Now I'm out on a limb,
And it looks pretty grim.
So how can I give you a high-five?

This dedication will have to do. Thanks, Tom.
You made this happen.

A Message for Adults

Writing this book reignited in me that childlike thrill of discovery. What started out as a book of silly limericks led me into the weird world of the creatures about which I was writing. Consequently, I decided to follow each limerick with a *What's the Scoop?* section. In it you'll find some unusual facts that many books don't cover about that animal. This book is not meant to be a substitute for more comprehensive reference books on animals. It will present information I found ironic, unusual, or extraordinary. Also, I sort through common myths and misconceptions about some of the animals. I hope you will use this book as a springboard to discuss the information with children. I suggest after reading each chapter, turning to the matching game for that chapter at the end of the book in the *What Did You Scoop Up?* section. The vocabulary will be a bit challenging, especially for young ones; but that's by design. I believe fun words make learning more enjoyable. Young children, 5 – 7, will probably only be interested in the limericks, but older kids (and adults) might be more fascinated by the information. The first entry for each chapter will contain supplementary information in a footnote about related topics, particularly about the scientific system of the classification of animals. It is designed to help kids understand and remember that system. I designed this book to be as much fun for you as it is for the kids. If you laugh half as much while reading it as I did while writing it, you better buckle up.

Contents

Rules for Reading Limericks — ix

Zoo Animals & Exotic Creatures — 10

Bugs, Spiders & Creeping Crawlers — 24

Birds from Around the World — 38

Pets & Domesticated Animals — 52

Wild Animals of the Americas — 66

What Did You Scoop Up? — 81

My purpose is to be a left-hand bookend, and I'm so excited. I'll keep track of the page you're on as we read through this book together.

When animals are born, within hours
They instinctively know their own powers.
But for you and I,
We've a lifetime to try
To discover what powers are ours.

This book is a bit peculiar. For example, it comes with bookends, a page counting bug, some questions and answers, and a set of rules. These rules are for your benefit and protection. Let's stay safe while reading. We don't want any limerick-reading related injuries.

Rules for Reading Limericks:

1. You **must** read a limerick out loud.
   Reading silently is not allowed.
   But beware, you might chuckle
   So hard you could buckle.
   So never read in a large crowd.

   (Did you just violate Rule 1? Let's try that again.)

2. If you are just playing around,
   One place you should never be found
   Is high up a tree
   With this book on your knee;
   You could find yourself flat on the ground.

   (Don't climb a tree with any book, especially this one.)

3. Like Mom always says, "Take care".
   So sit in a well-padded chair
   With pillows all 'round
   And feet on the ground,
   Then laugh as hard as you dare.

   (Helmets are optional.)

Sleepwalking can be hazardous to your health.

A giraffe has horns on its head,
So at night when it gets out of bed,
It lights up each horn,
So that it can warn
All airplanes by flashing bright red.

We're on page **11**

What's the Scoop?

Giraffe "horns" are stubby skin and hair covered outgrowths on their skulls called ossicones. No one knows what purpose they serve. They might help hold thorny branches away from a giraffe's face when it eats acacia tree leaves, its favorite food. But since that's only a guess, maybe they could be for holding warning lights. Some have speculated that they are for fighting, since that's how most animals use their horns. But giraffes fight with their muscular necks, not their stubby skull outgrowths. Giraffes are the tallest land animal and can reach heights about the same as a two-story house, nearly twenty feet, from the tips of their toes to the tops of their ossicones. Without the ossicones they would only be like 19½ feet tall. A collective noun* for a <u>herd</u> of giraffes is a <u>tower</u>. Also, the assumption that giraffes do not make vocal sounds is a myth. They do not have vocal chords, but they have been observed making guttural noises. Experts speculate that giraffes might communicate across long distances in a vocal range lower than human ears can hear. But what they say to each other is the real mystery. "OMG. Gertrude has her head stuck in the clouds again".

Collective nouns are words that label a group of things having common characteristics. Some examples of collective nouns for groups of animals are a <u>pride</u> of lions, a <u>pod</u> of dolphins, a <u>bevy</u> of quail, or a <u>swarm</u> of flies. In this book all collective nouns will be underlined, and we'll have fun with them. Some imaginative collective nouns for animals incorporate qualities of that animal, and they will show up in most "What's the Scoop?" sections of this book. Some people, especially those who love words, enjoy collective nouns. Lovers of words are called verbophiles, but that term often carries a negative nerdy connotation. Some verbophiles have a habit of excessively correcting other people's misuse of words. Don't do that; it only perpetuates the stereotype. I enjoy being a verbophile, and I want to encourage you to be one as well. There is not much practical use for most collective nouns. For example, how many groups of centipedes or porcupines have you seen? Sometimes these words have roots in Old English or foreign languages with an interesting story. The study of word origins is called etymology. (Verbophiles like words like etymology.) Collective nouns are frequently words that someone coined, often an author, and their continued use was popularized because people liked them. In a few places throughout this book, you will be encouraged to make up your own collective nouns. For example, I might call a group of word lovers a <u>thesaurus</u> of verbophiles. What would you call them?

Chimpanzees
can swing
from trees
Like acrobats
on a trapeze.
They have
lots of fun,
But when
they are done,
Their arms
hang down
to their knees.

Hmmm...

What's the Scoop?

Chimpanzees, or chimps, have arms longer than their legs—over half their body height. They are naturally acrobatic because they can grip with their feet as well as they can with their hands. Chimps can walk upright on the ground but are much more adept at swinging through the trees. That's where they live, eat, sleep, and develop other practical uses for really long arms. One collective noun for chimps is a <u>whoop</u>, and the collective noun for apes in general is a <u>shrewdness</u>. Apes are different from monkeys. Both are primates, but apes are larger and have no tail. Other types of apes are gorillas and orangutans. Monkeys, on the other hand, have long tails that may be used as a fifth limb. Some monkeys have a prehensile tail, which means they can grasp with it and hang upside down. A group of them can be as much fun to watch as a <u>barrel</u> of monkeys—one of their collective nouns. Now do you see how much fun collective nouns can be? Let me hear a big <u>whoop</u>.

Does this bow make my snout look bigger?

You needn't be told by a teacher
That a warthog's an ugly creature.
One glance at its snout
Will dispel any doubt,
And its snout is its handsomest feature.

What's the Scoop?

Warthog "warts" are not warts. They are large hard bumps on their face, snout, and elsewhere. The warts contain fatty tissue, similar to camel humps. Myth alert: neither camel humps nor warthog warts store water, just fat. The warts may also serve as protection, deflecting the tusks of other warthogs. Female warthogs seem to like them. Warthogs have an annoying habit of talking with food in their mouths. Thus, a collective noun for them is the same as that for all types of pigs and hogs, a <u>sounder</u>. Another collective noun alludes to the fact that male warthogs live alone, a <u>solitary</u>. But it seems silly to assign a collective noun to an animal claiming to be a group of one. They must have egos big enough for a whole <u>herd</u>.

When a gorilla wants you to be wary,
It'll beat on its chest and sound scary.
I'm very impressed,
'Cause it beats on its chest
So hard that its chest isn't hairy.

What's the Scoop?

Gorillas can weight over 500 pounds. They pound their chests not only to show aggression, but also to communicate. All that chest thumping probably does impede hair growth on those beefy pecs (pectoral muscles). Also, gorillas display uncanny ingenuity at problem solving and a wide range of human emotions. In the wild, they have been observed cooperatively dismantling poacher traps and grieving inconsolably over the loss of loved ones. One amazing ability of gorillas is they do not need to drink water; they get all the moisture they need from the vegetation they eat. A group of them is called a <u>band</u>. Perhaps the world's most famous gorilla was Koko. She was taught to communicate with humans by learning about 1000 words in sign language. I doubt the word *pecs* was on that list, but *please* and *thank you* probably were.

What was I supposed to do today?

An elephant remembers all
Its thoughts, no matter how small.
But I'd be more impressed
If you could suggest
One thing that it needs to recall.

What's the Scoop?

Elephants can live about 80 years. They have been observed remembering old friends and remote feeding locations after 30 years of separation. Two creative collective nouns for them are a <u>memory</u> and a <u>parade</u>, because elephants usually walk in single file. An elephant's nose is its most amazing feature. Also called a *proboscis*, but more often a trunk, it can bend in any direction and lift up to 600 pounds. It can also smell about 5000 times better than a human's nose, picking up odors from miles away. Elephants are the largest **land** animal, but not the largest over all. Male bulls typically weight over three tons or 6000 pounds, but they are dwarfed by the largest animal of all. It tips the scale at about 200 tons or 400,000 pounds—the blue whale. It would take about 66 elephants to equal one blue whale. Elephants like to forget that.

I was told we'd be taking the scenic route.

Gnus live in a place with a beautiful view,
But the view's only seen by a few.
Herds of gnus are so vast
That few can see past
The back end of some other gnu.

What's the Scoop?

Another name for a gnu (usually pronounced NEW, but sometimes ga-NEW) is a wildebeest. The name imitates the grunting noise they make. During migration about two million gnus are on the move in a massive earthshaking <u>implausibility</u> of gnus. They are referred to as the clowns of the savanna because, during mating season, they will be grazing calmly and suddenly jump up, spin around, roll in the dust, and gallop off and back again. Then just as suddenly, they stop and go back to grazing. Maybe spending so much time migrating in a massive <u>implausibility</u> with no view to stare at makes them go a little stir crazy.

If a cheetah asks to race when it meets ya,
Best decline, 'cause it's going to beat ya.
You better just face it,
If you chose to race it,
It may not only race ya, but eat ya.

What's the Scoop?

Cheetahs are the fastest **land** animal. (You'll find out the fastest overall later.) They can reach a top speed of about 75 miles per hour and accelerate from zero to 60 in about three seconds. The world's fastest human tops out at about 28 mph and goes from zero to 60 that quickly only in a really fast sports car. Cheetahs are built for speed, with small heads and lightweight bodies. They have extra-large hearts and lungs for fueling their muscles with plenty of oxygen and a flexible spine that acts like a spring propelling their powerful legs. The cheetah's bulky tail helps maintain its center of balance and facilitates crazy sharp turns. A family of cheetahs hunt together in a <u>coalition</u>. If you want to race a cheetah, better challenge it to a gunny sack race. No, that probably won't work. Maybe challenge it to a race where you carry an egg on a spoon. On second thought, don't play any competitive games with a cheetah. It might be a sore loser.

Air kisses are socially acceptable too.

What is the polite way to greet
An octopus when you meet?
I don't understand.
Do I offer my hand
Or offer both hands and both feet?

What's the Scoop?

Octopuses, or octopi, are really weird. They have eight arms, three hearts that pump blue blood, two gills for water jet propulsion, one sharp bird-like beak (the only hard part of its body), and zero bones. Most species have the amazing ability to change the color and shape of their skin for camouflage. They can curl up next to a rock and quickly change their color and shape to match it. They are reclusive and probably won't want to shake your hand, but if they offer, don't. They may ask for a big hug, but, trust me, you don't want one. Octopuses are seldom seen in groups, but nevertheless there is a collective noun for them: a <u>consortium</u>. When they've reached an agreement after consorting, I wonder how many handshakes it takes to seal the deal. Awkward.

It's good to be king.

The lion has high self-esteem.
But he's always asleep, it would seem.
He surely must bungle
Being king of the jungle.
If he's king, then he's king in his dreams.

What's the Scoop?

Lions can sleep up to twenty hours a day, and large adults can eat up to fifteen pounds of meat a day. That's like 60 quarter-pound hamburgers. A lion's daily routine breaks down to about four hours of hunting and eating, followed by twenty hours of resting and digesting all that red meat. There's not much time left for ruling the kingdom. The lion's roar can be heard by humans from over five miles away, but lion researchers observed one lion responding to the roar of a potential rival from 35 miles away. That's about as far as the distance you cover when riding in the car for over half an hour. With a roar like that, a lion can proclaim rule over its entire monarchy without cutting into nap time. Now that's a lot of pride.

I think it's a Teddy Koala.

Some so-called "bears" are in error.
A koala is not a bear.
A bearcat's not either.
In fact, it is neither
A bear nor a cat; so there.

What's the Scoop?

Perhaps the most popular toy of all time is the Teddy Bear. It first appeared in 1903 and was named after President Teddy Roosevelt after he spared the life of a bear on a hunting trip. The early versions of the toy bear looked more like a real bear, but later versions resembled a koala. Thus, koalas are often called bears, but they are marsupials, in the same family as kangaroos. The koala's most amazing feature is its ability to live by only eating eucalyptus leaves, which are toxic to most animals. Bearcats, or binturongs, are in the mongoose family— also not a bear. The number of schools that have a Bearcat mascot exceeds the number of bearcats in existence. Bearcats are in extreme danger of extinction. Only a handful of sightings have been made in recent years. There are no collective nouns for koalas or bearcats, but a collection of teddy bears is called a <u>hug</u>. Ahhhh.

Kangaroos can jump to the sky.
So they think they're in charge from on high.
If one says, "Hop to it!";
Then you better do it;
And salute and answer, "Aye aye!"

What's the Scoop?

Two of the collective nouns for a group of kangaroos are a <u>mob</u> or a <u>troop</u>. Kangaroos like to fight, and when they do, it's like cage fighting—anything goes. They box and scratch with their front arms, but they can also use their tails for balance and leverage to deliver knockout blows with their powerful hind legs and giant feet. If a kangaroo orders you to jump, don't ask how high because kangaroos can leap higher and farther than any other animal—up to 6 feet high and over 25 feet long. The human world record holder for a standing jump is over 5 feet high (but most people can jump about 2 feet) and for a standing long jump, a little over 12 feet. If kangaroos were in the military, they'd probably all be drill sergeants. They wouldn't march in unison, but they'd keep the <u>troop</u> hopping.

Hippos think all fat is luggable.
That's why they look so huggable.
But they're not a plush toy;
They're easy to annoy.
To hippos you only look muggable.

What's the Scoop?

A common collective noun for hippopotami is a <u>bloat</u>, which is what you feel when you overeat. There are more hippo attacks on people than any other **land** animal. Just because they're plant eaters doesn't mean they're not mean. Their lower tusks can grow up to about two feet long, and the upper and lower tusks align at an angle so they sharpen each other. They can open their mouths nearly four feet wide. (How tall are you?) Hippos can also run surprisingly fast, both underwater and on land. They can spend up to 16 hours a day in the water and can stay submerged for up to six minutes before coming up for air. Here's the weird part: they sleep underwater and resurface for air without waking up. They usually only leave the water at night to forage for grass and fruit. The most unusual characteristic of hippos is that they sweat a red fluid. It's called *blood sweat* because people used to think it was blood, but it's a unique acid that acts as a sunscreen and lotion for their skin. I'm guessing it must be about SPF 80, for I've never seen a sunburned hippo. There's an internet myth that hippo milk is pink. It isn't, but I'm glad I'm not the one who had to milk a hippo to find that out!

Bugs, Spiders & Creeping Crawlers

June bugs hit walls and then
Will fly up and hit them again.
That could explain why
Whenever they fly
They never know where they have been.

What's the Scoop?

Yes, this is a book about animals, and, yes, June bugs are animals. They are beetles, and all insects, spiders, and other creepy crawlers are in the animal kingdom. Life on Earth is scientifically classified on a seven-level system starting with kingdom and ending with species*. Kingdom separates all living things into plants and animals. So, when I refer to *animals* in this book, I simply mean they are in the animal kingdom. The scientific ranking below kingdom is phylum, which separates animals as either having an internal backbone (vertebrate) or an exoskeleton (invertebrate or arthropod). All the animals in this chapter are invertebrates. There are more species of beetle than any other animal, about 400,000 out of about 1.3 million known animal species (at the time of this writing). That does not mean there are more beetles than any other animal, only that there are more different types of beetles than there are different types of any other animal. Beetles represent over one-fourth of all animal species, and almost all of them cannot maneuver very well in flight. For clarity, all beetles have wings, or remnants of wings, but not all can fly. There are so many different types of beetles that generalized statements need to be qualified with many exceptions. However, there is no exception for the name of a group: a colony. There's a lot of head banging going on with beetles. Fortunately, they all wear full body armor, and most have small heads, which may be because they've been banged so much.

Species is the last of seven main rankings in the taxonomic classification system for biological life. Species represents the varieties of one kind of animal that is able to reproduce its own kind. Consider the many different varieties of dogs: Akitas, Basset Hounds, Beagles, Boxers, Bulldogs, Chihuahuas, Cocker Spaniels, Collies, and that's just a few from A to C. There are over 500 breeds of domesticated dogs. Domesticated dogs are actually a subspecies, not a species; but they are a good example that one kind of animal can have many diverse characteristics. Worldwide about 10,000 new species are discovered every year, and scientists believe there are approximately 7.5 million more undiscovered species. Many of these are in places very difficult to reach, such as the bottom of the ocean or remote regions of rain forests. Many more are so small they can only be discovered with microscopes. But the final total of diversity of life on earth could be nearly nine million species. We don't know as much as we think we do about the animals with whom we share our planet. But what we do know is utterly amazing, and doesn't that make you wonder what we'll find out about the millions of undiscovered species?

We're on page 26

Now all I need is a marshmallow and a stick.

At night a moth always goes
Where the brightest and warmest light glows.
It's every moth's plight
To be cold at night,
For they eat up all their warm clothes.

What's the Scoop?

Adult moths don't eat clothes. That's a myth. In fact, many don't eat anything at all. Some adult moths don't even have mouths. They don't live very long either. The adult moth's life cycle typically only lasts long enough to mate and lay eggs. The worm-like larvae that hatch from those eggs will eat whatever food source is nearby, even if it is your favorite sweater or another item of clothing with natural fibers. Moth larvae won't eat synthetic fibers, such as nylon or rayon. Those probably taste like the raw material they're made from—oil. Many animals go through a larval stage before they transform into adults. Finally, there is disagreement over which is the largest moth in the world; both the Atlas Moth and the Hercules Moth have wingspans of nearly a foot, almost as wide as this book. A collective noun for moths is a <u>whisper</u>, rather ironic for those with no mouths.

A centipede really can haul,
Moving dozens of legs in all;
And I can tell
How it does so well.
It doesn't have far to fall.

What's the Scoop?

The prefix *centi-* means one hundred and *pede* means legs, but, oddly enough, no centipede has exactly 100 legs. Different species have between 15 and 177 pairs of legs, one pair for each body segment, for a total of 30 – 354 legs. However, their body segments always add up to an odd number. So, no centipede would have exactly 100 legs because none would have exactly 50 body segments, an even number. Centipedes have poisonous venom—on their front pincers. Also, most centipedes continue to grow additional body segments as adults, completely unique in the insect world. If they lose some legs, they will grow back. Their legs move in a wave-like motion when they walk, so it appears that they do not move independently. One rogue leg could easily throw off the rhythm of all the others. That would be like one wrong move by a high kicking dancer in a Broadway chorus line bringing down the whole row. I'd like to see a chorus line featuring one giant centipede. Now that would be a sure Broadway hit—so long as it didn't attack the audience, like King Kong. There is no collective noun for centipedes, but I'd go with a <u>sprint</u>. What can you come up with?

Ha, Ha! You can't catch me.

"Don't run on the table, my son".
Mom says, "That just isn't done".
So I'll slouch in my chair
And think how unfair
That flies get to have all the fun.

What's the Scoop?

House flies don't run for fun, they fly. Their wings beat about 200 times per second. Very impressive, but that buzzing sound is certainly annoying. Each of a fly's eyes has over 4000 lenses, thus making them very hard to sneak up on and swat. Flies can carry bacteria because they frequently feed on decaying matter. Every pile of dog poo almost immediately becomes a fly magnate. Flies have taste receptors on their feet that lets them know when they land on something edible. Then they vomit digestive juices on it, so they can suck up the liquefied gunk with sponge-like mouths. Gross. They live a month or two, unless you can swat them sooner. A <u>swarm</u> of them is called a <u>business</u>, which is somewhat creative because it sounds like buzz. But there's got to be a more descriptive collective noun. Perhaps a <u>grossness</u> or a <u>vomit</u> of flies. Any thoughts?

Tarantulas don't need to be brave.
They're so big they don't have to behave.
They look really weird.
Their whole body's a beard,
And no one will give them a shave.

What's the Scoop?

Tarantulas are the largest of all spiders, or arachnids. And the largest species of tarantula is the Goliath Bird-Eater. It can grow to about a foot long, large enough to cover a whole Frisbee (but it would be much harder to toss). Oddly enough the Goliath Bird Eater hardly lives up to its name. It usually catches and eats other insects, and occasionally frogs, rodents, bats, and small snakes. But birds are much harder to catch. Truth be told, most tarantulas are much less threatening than they appear. They have venom, but it's less potent than many other spiders. Still, their fangs can give a painful bite. They don't catch their prey in a web like many other spiders, they pounce on them at night. Tarantulas use the silk they spin to line their burrows or make a nest. They also have a unique defense against predators, small critters and birds of prey. They have sharp barbed hairs on the underside of their abdomen, which they can rub off with their hind legs and flick at the predator. If these barbed hairs hit soft tissue or eyes, they can be extremely painful. The most amazing feature of tarantulas is that not only do they shed and replace their exoskeleton, they can also regrow some internal organs and legs when they molt. The new leg may be shorter than the others at first, but gets progressively longer each time the spider sheds its exoskeleton. Any group of spiders is called a <u>cluster</u>, but there is no universally accepted collective noun for tarantulas. Can you come up with a good one? I'm kind of partial to a <u>stubble</u> of tarantulas.

I come out to enjoy the rain, and the ground turns into concrete.

Worms dig in the dirt with pride,
But they surely could use a guide.
They're not very brainy,
Because when it's rainy
They're stranded on sidewalks and dried.

What's the Scoop?

Worms don't have a brain, but they do have a rudimentary nervous system for detecting light, which they avoid. They appear to be little more than a digestion tract with a mouth at one end and a hole at the other, but there's more to them than that. They don't have lungs, so they breathe through their skin. When they dry out, they can't breathe. They have a strange reproductive system wrapped around their middle. After mating, this band slides off, filled with eggs. Worms are greatly valued by gardeners. They fertilize and aerate the soil, eating about their own weight in organic matter every day. It's estimated that there's an average of about a million worms on every acre of land on Earth. The largest worm ever found was 22 feet long, in South Africa. (I have no idea how old it was, but that's a lot of growth for something that only eats dirt.) Worms don't have a clue. The only place you'll find a group of them is in a fisherman's bait box. Guess what the collective noun for that is: a <u>clew</u>. That's an Old English word meaning a tangled ball, as of yarn or rope. I wonder if a <u>clew</u> of clueless worms ever got so big they couldn't figure out how to untangle themselves.

A dragonfly never cries
Because of the size of its eyes.
It probably fears
A flood of its tears
Could drown it before it flies.

What's the Scoop?

Each eye of a dragonfly has about 30,000 lenses, for a total of 60,000 eyes and 360° vision. That's about the same number of eyes as are in a filled major league baseball stadium. Dragonflies use about 80% of their brain to process all that visual input, whereas we only use about 20% of our brains. Also, dragonflies have no equal when it comes to putting on aerobatic displays. They have two sets of independently rotatable wings. So they can fly straight up and down, make sharp U-turns at full speed, and fly upside down. A dragonfly's maneuverability is so complex it exceeds the limits of man's ability to duplicate with robotics. The collective noun that best recognizes these unique abilities is a <u>flight</u>, but they can also be called a <u>cluster</u>. Finally, don't worry, dragonflies wouldn't drown even if they could cry. They float on the surface of water. Go ahead, look a dragonfly right in the eye—pick one—and wave a freshly cut onion in front of it. But be sure to have lots of tiny tissues on hand.

Stop it. I don't have to go.

When I see a spider,
I brush it,
'Cause Mom doesn't like me
to crush it.
To her it's an issue,
So with a clean tissue,
It's dropped in the toilet
to flush it.

What's the Scoop?

All spiders, except one family, are venomous; but only a few species, such as the Black Widow and Brown Recluse, can be harmful (or even deadly) to people. In fact, one collective noun for them is a <u>venom</u>. Most books explain that spiders, which are arachnids, differ from insects because they have two body parts instead of three and eight legs instead of six. However, less commonly explained is that most spiders also have eight eyes. Some have more, and a few have fewer. Each of their eyes is adapted to see different depths and locations. Additionally, all spiders have the ability to produce silk strands. However, they don't all weave webs with their silk. Some spiders use the fibers for other purposes—such as escaping from being flushed down the toilet. If you could weave enough strands of spider silk to make it the same size as a steel rod and put both through a stress test, the steel would break before the flexible silk strand. There are probably thousands of spiders living in your house right now, but you don't see them because they usually like dark places, and most are very small. One spider can lay over 7000 eggs during its typical two-year lifecycle. There aren't enough names for all their offspring, but every spider assumes it must be *Eek!*

Go ahead. Call me a lady one more time.

Not all ladybugs you see
Are girls, and I think maybe
It surely annoys
Those that are boys
To always be called a "she".

What's the Scoop?

Ladybugs, also called ladybirds or ladybeetles, were named after the Virgin Mary—Our Lady. During the Middle Ages in Europe, crops were being devastated; and farmers prayed to Mary for help. They believed their prayers were answered by the appearance of little red and black spotted beetles that ate aphids and other crop destroying pests. So, male ladybugs take heart; you're not being called female, but blessed. The ladybug's bright coloration is actually a warning to potential predators. As a defense against being eaten, ladybugs can secrete an obnoxious smelly substance from their leg joints that tastes awful. It must be really bad stuff if birds won't eat it; birds will eat anything. Ladybugs are a popular design for kids' toys, clothing, jewelry, backpacks, and so on. A collection of ladybug paraphernalia, as well as a collection of ladybugs, is a <u>loveliness</u>. That word obviously doesn't take into account they can emit smelly stuff from their joints.

My mom does
the craziest
dance
When she sees
a trail of ants
Marching over
the floor
To the pantry
door.
You'd think
she had ants
in her pants.

Hurry up. She's a stomper.

What's the Scoop?

Ants can lift 100 times their own body weight—or more. But they only weight about three milligrams on average. People weigh about a million times more than that. However, in the world there are about a million times more ants than people. So all totaled, ants and people account for about the same total mass on the planet. If 10,000 ants could figure out a way to lift you, you'd find yourself slowly moving over the ground toward an ant <u>colony</u>. Doesn't that make you want to do a crazy dance? Also, ants have too many legs to march in unison, but they are still called an <u>army</u>—and they don't even stop and salute.

He always picks the same place to hide—under that stupid shell.

Don't play hide and seek with a snail.
You must count too long without fail.
And then when you seek,
You need only peek
'Neath the shell at the end of its trail.

What's the Scoop?

Snails have the reputation for being the slowest animal on Earth. At full throttle, they max out at about 50 yards an hour. A six-year-old could run that far while the snail was still crossing the starting line, and a turtle could beat a snail by about 49 yards in a 50-yard race. Also, snails might be a bit old to play hide and seek; some species live up to 25 years. A collective noun for snails is a <u>rout</u>. an obsolete spelling of route, meaning a trail or path—but not necessarily of slime. That slime is their most amazing feature. It can be both slippery and sticky like glue, allowing snails to glide straight up walls. Also, snails can make their slimy mucus so thick they can glide over the upraised edge of a razor blade without being cut. Now that's a real super power. Do **not** try that at home.

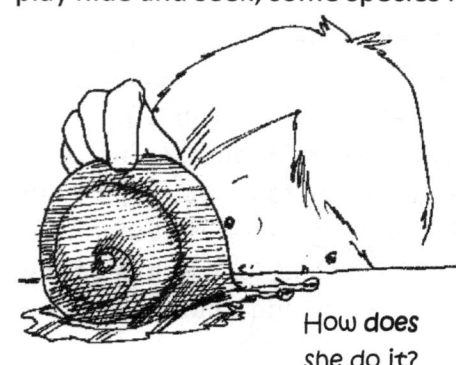

How **does** she do it?

This limerick is a riddle. Try to figure it out before reading the answer in *What's the Scoop?*

The deadliest animal's not grand.
It's one you might misunderstand.
It's found everywhere,
And can bite unaware.
Yet you could kill it with one hand.

What's the Scoop?

This animal causes the deaths of over one million people a year. That's over 5000 times the number of deaths caused by **all** other animal bites combined. These deaths are not due to the bite itself, but to diseases that might result. Have you figured it out? By far, the deadliest animal on earth is also one of the smallest—the mosquito. They must lay their eggs in standing water. But they can fly about twenty miles and live about two months. If they are within 75 yards of you, they can detect your presence by the carbon dioxide you exhale. Hundreds of millions of dollars are spent annually controlling mosquito populations and hundreds of millions more on researching and treating the diseases they spread, making it also the costliest animal on the planet to control. However, there is another animal that historically has been even more deadly—one that is usually excluded from this list because it is considered to be above the animals. It's man. Human history is a constant record of one war after another, yet everyone would say they want peace. We need to learn how to achieve that.

I'll just carry this trophy for you.

The peregrine's an amazing bird,
About which you may not have heard.
It flutters up high,
Then dives down to fly
At speeds that are really absurd.

What's the Scoop?

How absurd is the peregrine falcon? It's the fastest animal on Earth. When it goes into a dive, called a stoop, it can reach speeds up to 240 mph. Other birds of prey, or raptors, such as eagles and hawks, can reach speeds over 200 mph in a stoop; but the peregrine is the fastest. Skydivers usually fall at speeds about half that. The peregrine is designed to withstand that speed. It has air deflectors over its nostrils to avoid damaging its lungs and a third eyelid to moisturize the eye and keep it from drying out while diving. Also, the peregrine's eyes are designed to stay focused on one object when they are moving at top speed. Have you ever tried to focus on a nearby object while riding in the car driving down the highway? When a peregrine pulls out of a dive, it can endure a g-force* of about ten. Some people pass out if they experience a g-force around five (or less), causing blood to drain from their heads. Now tell me that's not an absurd bird. The peregrine is one of many birds popularly trained for falconry, an ancient sport where birds are captured and taught to hunt in the wild and return to their handler. Although modern falconers are perhaps not as prevalent as in previous centuries many people are still drawn to the lure of vicariously participating in the phenomenal feats of these raptors. Falconry requires a large commitment of time and money, beginning with a two-year apprenticeship under a licensed Master Falconer. The peregrine was put on the endangered species list in 1970, but was taken off in 1999, in large part because of the efforts of committed falconers to prevent the bird's extinction from becoming reality. Birds with these abilities are definitely worth saving.

One g is the gravitational force determining how much you weigh right now. If you normally weigh 100 pounds and were standing on a scale while enduring a force of 10 g's, the scale would read 1000 pounds. Of course, you would not be standing very long because your legs are not strong enough to sustain that much weight. Also, if that amount of g-force continued, your body would literally crush itself. Fighter pilots are physically trained to endure brief pulls of around 9 g's. Also, extreme rollercoasters are rated for the maximum g-force riders will experience, with several rated around 5 g's. They require riders to be in good health. If you have ever experienced the feeling of weightlessness in a falling ride at a theme park or in high altitude flight, that would be 0 g's. The quickest way to lose weight is to stand on a scale while at 0 g's. Of course, you would gain back all that weight as soon as you got back to the real world.

I was just standing around minding my own business and...

A flock of ravens is named
A *murder*, for they often get blamed
For disturbing the peace.
Then they'll never cease
Saying, "It wasn't me. I was framed".

What's the Scoop?

A <u>murder</u> really is one of the collective nouns for flocks of ravens or crows. Those two birds are often mixed up because they look similar. Ravens are larger, but unless you see them side by side, it's hard to tell. Ravens are also one of the smartest of all animal species. In captivity they can learn to mimic human speech better than parrots, and they become quite good at making excuses for bad behavior. A couple other collective nouns are an <u>unkindness</u> and a <u>storytelling</u>. The word a raven is most famous for saying is "Nevermore", which it repeatedly speaks in Edgar Allan Poe's macabre poem *The Raven*. Poe lived in Baltimore, and that poem became the inspiration for the name of the only professional football team ever named after a poem, the Nightingales... No, that's not right, the Baltimore Ravens.

Here's lookin' at you, kid.

To show that his love is true
What a courting peacock will do
Is fan out his tail,
Then tell the female
I only have eyes for you.

What's the Scoop?

A peacock's tail feathers are iridescent, changing color as light hits them at different angles. Only male birds are called peacocks; females are peahens. The males will fan out their tails to attract females, who might say, "The way the light hits your tail, I think you're winking at me". The spots on a peacock's tail that look like eyes are called *ocelli*. In fact, any design resembling an eye, such as a spot within a circle, can be called an ocellus. A gathering of peacocks trying to attract the attention of a peahen is an <u>ostentation</u>. If you have ever described someone as being "stuck up", you're using a term originally applied to the way peacocks looked when they stuck up their tail feathers. Many other types of male birds attempt to attract females with beautiful songs, but the peacock's call is such an annoying squawk that not even peahens are attracted to it. Smart peacocks learn to zip it and let their eyes do the talking.

The penguins,
as a whole,
Live near
the cold
South Pole.
I wonder if
That's why
they're so stiff
Whenever
they go
for a stroll.

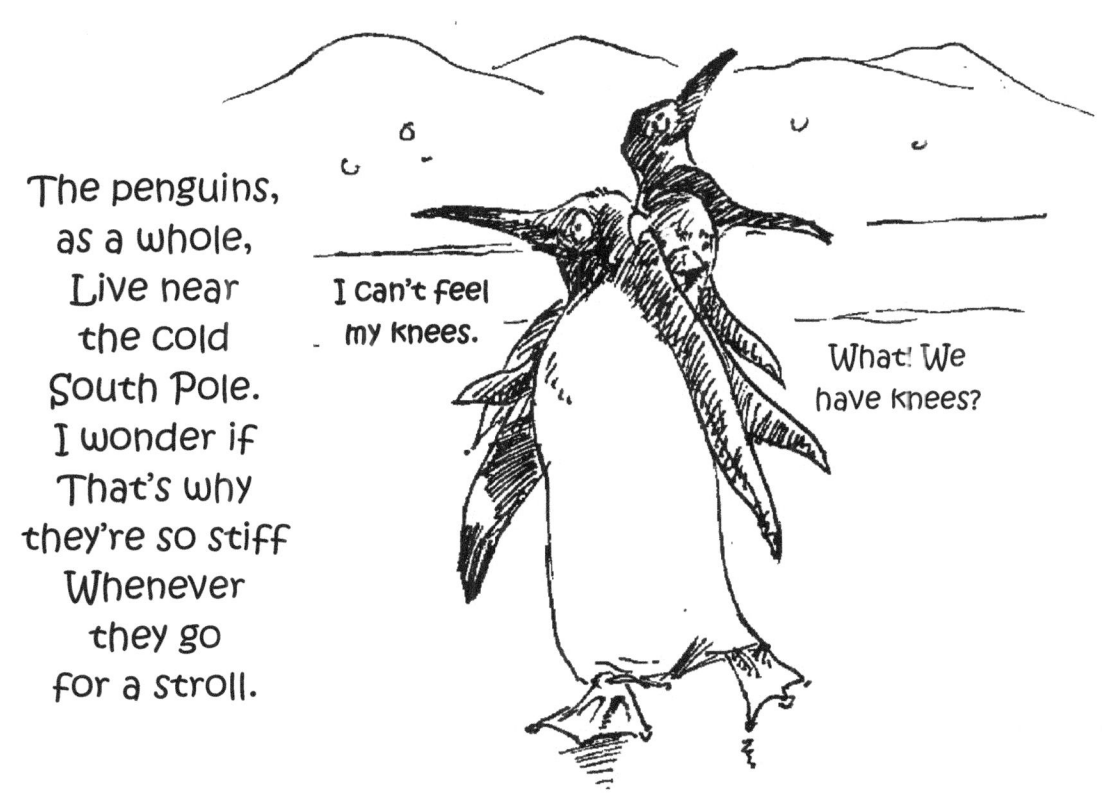

"I can't feel my knees."

"What! We have knees?"

What's the Scoop?

Almost all penguins live in the Southern Hemisphere, but not just in Antarctica. Some people have speculated that penguins waddle because they have no knees, but that's not the case. Penguins are designed to be more adept at swimming in water than walking on land. You could easily outrun a penguin, but you could never outswim one. Their black and white coloration and stiff demeanor has led to describing formal tuxedos as penguin suits. A gathering of penguins is a <u>rookery</u>, a word that literally means a breeding ground. But penguins do more than that in their <u>rookery</u>. Mom and Dad will take turns incubating their egg while the other goes out for food. When the eggs hatch, the parents take turns raising their chick. The harsh difficulties of growing up as a penguin has inspired many documentary filmmakers, and animated ones as well. Penguins may not have happy knees, but some have very happy feet.

During hunting season you'll see
Ducks flying o'er land and sea.
To show that they're brave,
They'll always wave
A "V" for victory!

"Quack-quack" means
a little help here!

What's the Scoop?

Ducks, geese, and other birds migrate thousands of miles every year, flying in a V formation, called a skein. That way the bird in front provides extra lift for the one behind. The bird following flies about a meter behind and a meter to one side of the bird in front. The wind spins off the wing tips of the front duck in a vortex, a circular pattern where the air spirals off the wingtips in a horizontal eddy. Amazingly, the trailing duck times its wing flaps to hit the upward side of this vortex and thus gets extra lift. Squadrons of airplanes fly in this formation for a similar reason. They get better fuel efficiency by riding the updraft off the wing of the plane in front, without having to time the wing flaps. The point bird works the hardest, so it periodically drops back and lets the next in line take point. There are many collective nouns for ducks. On the water they're called a paddling or a raft, but hunters favor the word plump. Winston Churchill was the first to use the hand sign of a "V" for victory during World War II. The ducks assumed he was waving at them and have been waving back ever since.

Go team!

Heads up! This limerick is a bit of a tongue twister. Try reading it fast.

If I kick any higher, I'll fall off.

If one toucan the cancan can do,
Then two toucans can cancan too.
Add one or two more
To the dancehall floor,
For a toucan cancan revue.

What's the Scoop?

The cancan is a dance featuring lots of high kicking and petticoat waving. Needless to say, toucans can't cancan. But the words make a good tongue twister. Toucans are known for having the largest bills of all birds relative to their body size. Their brightly colored bills grow to about eight inches, about half the length of the rest of their body. But despite that, their bills are not as heavy as you might expect. A toucan's bill is not as dense and heavy as the beaks of most birds. Inside it's a sponge-like honeycombed material—mostly empty space. If the bill were denser, the toucan would be too top-heavy to fly; and they can't fly very far as it is. One collective noun for toucans is a <u>durante</u>. That might not be funny to you, but it would probably make your grandparents chuckle. Jimmy Durante was a comedian in a less politically correct time. He referred to himself as the Schnoz for his extra-large nose, and he had a lot of fun with it too.

The bald eagle should really be called
Anything other than bald.
Its head isn't bare;
There's feathers up there.
At calling it bald, I'm appalled.

What's the Scoop?

Bald eagles obviously have white feathers covering their heads. They are called bald because the Old English word *balde* means white. When you consider they could have been called towheaded or hoary headed eagles, the name *bald* eagle sounds pretty good. Any other name would not be majestic enough for the national symbol of the United States of America. Although they are not the largest bird in North America, they are the largest raptor, or bird of prey. The term *eagle eye* is used to describe anything with uncanny vision. Soaring eagles can spot a rabbit from as far as two miles away. Some eagles have a territory that covers 100 square miles. Thus they must put their visual acuity to good use. A group of them is an <u>aerie</u>, which is also the name for their nests. So that means a group of eagles nesting in the same area (which they don't) would be an <u>aerie</u> of aeries.

My etiquette coach said using silverware and a napkin is good table manners.

The baldest birds in the air,
On whose tops there's not much there,
Are vultures who eat
Nothing but meat;
And they like their meat very rare.

What's the Scoop?

Vultures, many species anyway, have bald heads because they stick them in their food. They are nature's waste disposal system, cleaning up dead carcasses that would otherwise blight the environment. They can detect methane gas emitted by carrion from more than a mile away. Natural gas companies use vultures to detect methane leaks in their pipelines. Vultures will circle around the location of the gas leak, hoping for a really big meal that they are never quite able to find. A <u>wake</u> refers to a group of vultures feeding; a <u>kettle</u> to a group circling in flight; and a <u>committee</u> or a <u>venue</u> to a group hanging around waiting for something to die. Also, the largest flying bird in the world is a vulture, the Andean Condor, some of which have a wingspan of over ten feet. That's longer than the distance from the floor to the ceiling of your house. They need really large wings because they can weigh over thirty pounds, about as much as the average toddler. That's pretty heavy to be held up by thin air and no jet engine. So they live near mountains and conserve energy by gliding on wind currents—while crying out, "Bald is beautiful".

We're on page 47

Hang a stethoscope around your neck, and everyone thinks you're a doctor.

A stork should fulfill one condition
Before bringing a new addition.
To deliver a baby,
A stork should maybe
First be an obstetrician.

What's the Scoop?

A common way of answering a young child's question "Where do babies come from?" used to be an evasive statement that storks brought them. That tradition started in Europe in the Middle Ages. Storks would return in the spring and build nests on rooftops and chimneys at a time when many babies were being born. A gathering of them is a word that means causing to gather— <u>mustering</u>. Storks catch minnows and fish by sticking their open bills in the water. They wait for a fish to brush it, then snap their bill shut in about 25 milliseconds. (A thousand milliseconds make one second.) Although difficult to rank, that reaction time is nearly unmatched by any other animal. By the way, storks couldn't make it through medical school. So, if a stork ever offers to deliver your baby, ask for a second opinion.

The ostrich is truly grand.
It's the buffest bird in the land.
So when it sees a threat,
Why does it fret
And bury its head in the sand?

What's the Scoop?

Ostriches can sprint about forty miles per hour, kick hard enough to kill a lion, stand about nine feet tall, and do **not** bury their heads in the sand when they sense danger. That's a myth. They are the tallest and fastest running birds in the world. They lay the largest eggs, have the largest eyes, and have valuable plumage and leather. Unfortunately, because of those last qualities, poachers have hunted them so much they are on the endangered species list. Ostriches can't outrun a bullet. You could say they are the other king of the jungle, and guess what a group of them is called: a <u>pride</u>. They have the same collective noun as lions, and ostriches don't have to sleep most of the day.

My brain keeps hammering even after my head stops.

A woodpecker only
gets fed
By beating its beak
with its head.
It can hammer
quite hard
Without
getting jarred,
But its head does get
bright red.

What's the Scoop?

Not all woodpeckers have red heads, but they can make up to 20 pecks in the time it takes you to say "Woody Woodpecker" (1 second). See how many times you can tap your finger in one second, and then try to imagine how fast you would have to do it to hit 20. On a busy day, woodpeckers might tap up to 12,000 times. That's a lot of headbanging, but they have reinforced skulls and a gel-like cushion around their brains, so they can handle it. Also, when their long tongue is retracted, it wraps around the backs of their brains to act as an extra cushion. Woodpeckers do not make vocal sounds, but tap to communicate. Because their tapping sounds like the rata-tat-tat of a machine gun, a <u>flock</u> can be called a <u>gatling</u>, which is the name of the forerunner of the machine gun. But a woodpecker's tapping is much faster than the original Gatling gun. Woodpeckers can tap about 1200 times per minute, and a Gatling gun could only fire about 400 rounds per minute—and that was with 10 barrels and no brains.

A pink flamingo asleep
Will tuck itself into a heap.
It looks like an egg
Balanced high on one leg.
Laws of physics, it seems not to keep.

What's the Scoop?

Several water birds sleep while standing on one leg, but flamingos look particularly strange because their bodies are so large and their legs so long and thin. Another odd behavior is the way flamingos eat. Wading in shallow water, they stir up mud and scrape the tops of their bills—upside down—across the water bed. They pump water in and out through special openings, then they sift out food with their sponge-like tongues. Plastic flamingos have long been a popular lawn ornament, perhaps because they look so flamboyant. A <u>flock</u> of them, whether real or plastic, is called a <u>flamboyance</u>. That's a word with an interesting etymology. Flamboyance is derived from a French word meaning a fiery blaze, and flamingos are so named because of their coloration. In *Alice's Adventures in Wonderland*, Alice learns flamingos make poor croquet mallets when she tries to play a game with the Queen of Hearts. The flamingo would look up quizzically as Alice tried to hit the ball with its head, and the hedgehog ball would scurry away as she tried to straighten the flamingo's neck. Through it all, the Queen kept shouting. I'm trying to remember, what did she say?

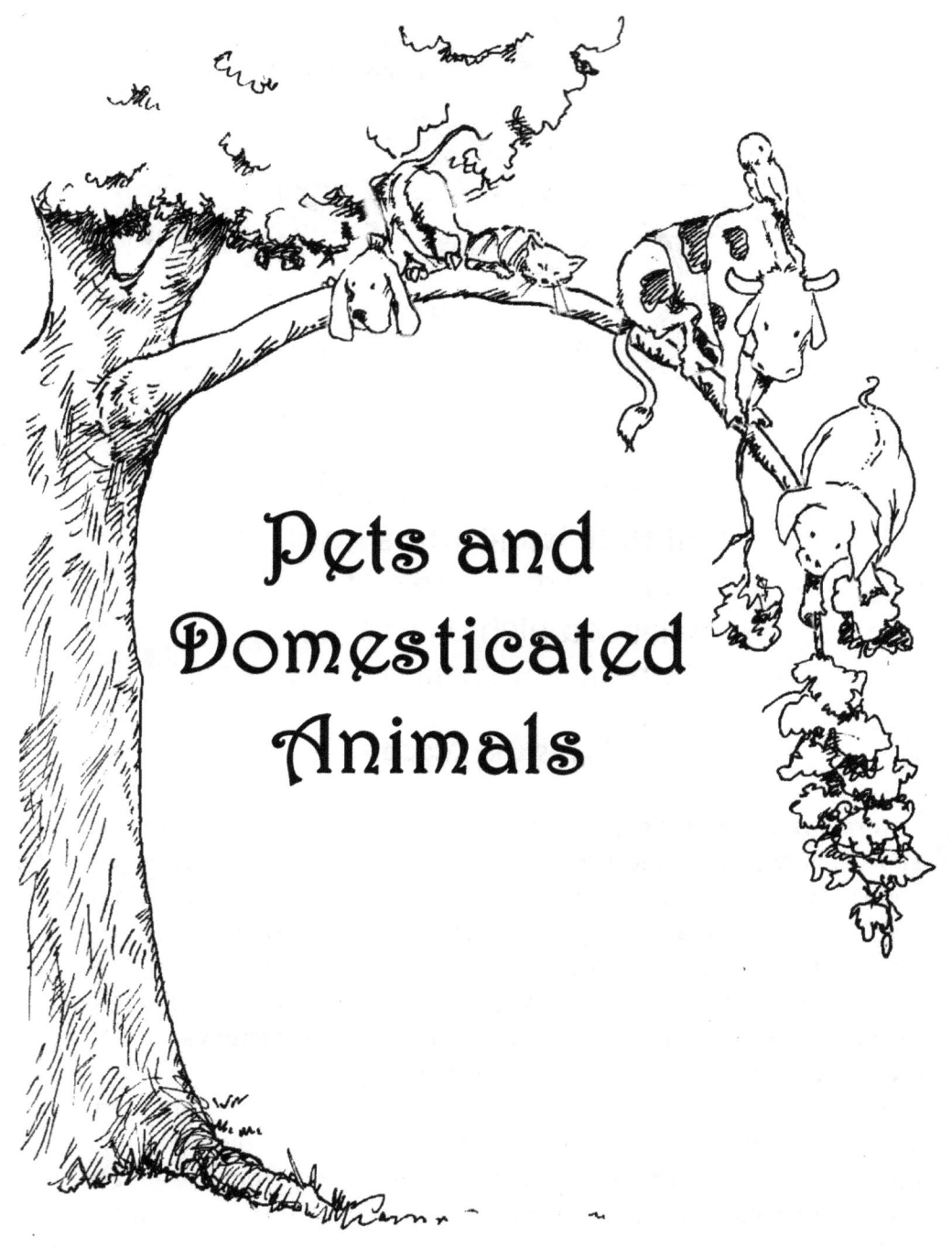

Please hug me. I brought your medicine.

A rabbit won't wheeze or sneeze.
It can breathe through its nose with ease.
Just how, I'm not sure,
Because its fur
Is bad for allergies.

What's the Scoop?

The popularity of pet animals goes through faddish cycles, but the Easter holiday often produces a bumper crop of pet bunnies. Although the Christian holiday celebrates resurrection and victory over death, the name Easter is rooted in an ancient pagan holiday celebrating fertility. That's why we have an Easter Bunny. Rabbits have always been a symbol of fertility. They can reproduce three or four times a year in litters of around three to eight. And female offspring can be ready to reproduce in as little as four months. Thus the offspring of a single pair of rabbits and the offspring of their offspring could produce well over 1000 new bunnies in less than two years, and that number goes hyperbolic in subsequent years. Now that's fertility. The most common collective noun for rabbits is a <u>warren</u>, a word that originally meant an enclosed area for breeding rabbits or other animals. Also, myth alert, you're not allergic* to their fur. Really, you're not. But that still doesn't mean you can stop sneezing around them.

---

*Animal fur itself is not what causes most allergic reactions. This is the case with all furry pets—cats, dogs, guinea pigs, rats, hamsters, and so on. Rather, people are allergic to other nasty stuff that gets on the fur. Animal fur can easily get contaminated with proteins from saliva, urine, and sweat. Also, microscopic mites living on skin flakes or pet dander can cause allergic reactions. You may be able to live with these allergens for years without being affected, but for some reason your body may unpredictably decide it has had enough and start reacting. Once the body's immune system identifies something as threatening, it attacks the invader by producing histamines, proteins designed to attack unwanted substances. A runny nose, sneezing, itchy skin, and watery eyes are your body's attempt to get rid of the allergen. Over half the homes in the U.S. have pets—over 160 million of them. About one-fifth, or 20 percent, of all pet owners have allergies. That's about 320,000 people. Yet, for the love of their pet, most of them choose to endure the allergy symptoms. That's a lot of runny noses, itchy rashes, and scratchy throats for love. It's also good for the sale of allergy medications. Hundreds of millions of pet owners literally experience the meaning of "love hurts".

I've yet to meet
a cat
Who never has
fancied that
It owned
the place
And by
its grace
Allowed us to be
where it's at.

You may stay.

What's the Scoop?

Cats have had a god complex for thousands of years. They were worshipped as gods by ancient Egyptians and have subsequently had to settle for being treated as royalty—a step down from godhood. The myth that cats have nine lives probably came from the Egyptian sun god who could take the form of a cat and birthed eight other gods. That myth has been popularized because cats seem to have an uncanny ability to escape unharmed from dangerous situations. Cats mark you as their subject by rubbing against you, leaving their scent. When they lick themselves, they're trying to get your scent off. In pop culture, fertile ground for new entries in the dictionary, snooty people are described as having *cattitude*. A cat's purring is its most amazing attribute. The low rumble of a purr resonates at a frequency that is believed to be healing and therapeutic, for both the cat and its human. Lastly, describing an impossible task is said to be "like trying to herd cats". Cats are not doggies. For that matter, doggies are not doggies either. A doggie is a word for a calf, particularly one being herded in a cattle drive. The collective noun for cats is a <u>clowder</u>, an Old English version of <u>clutter</u>. It's hard to herd a <u>clutter</u>.

She always serves the same thing for dessert.

There's nothing a goat ever ate
That it didn't think tasted great.
No need to do dishes,
A goat eats what it wishes,
And when done, it will eat up the plate.

What's the Scoop?

Goats being eating machines is mostly myth. They're usually picky eaters, but they often chew things to learn more about them, especially young kids. No, they don't chew children, young goats are called kids. Fainting goats achieved internet fame by toppling over with their legs stiff as a board when they were frightened. That's not a hoax; some goats have a condition called myotonia, a verbophile approved word for muscle paralysis, when they panic. Although they're called fainting goats, that's inaccurate. The goats don't really faint. They are fully conscious and breathe normally while in that condition. After a short time, their muscles relax enough for them to get up and continue doing whatever they were doing. However, that unusual condition might be the reason why one of the collective nouns for them is a <u>trip</u>.

Yikes! You're not the mailman.

My dog will lie on his mat
And bark at the mailman and cat.
But if he sees a stranger,
He only thinks danger;
And fast as he can, he will scat.

What's the Scoop?

Dogs have earned the title "Man's Best Friend" because they have a long history of service and loyalty to their owners. Just because one is occasionally a *scaredy cat* (dogs like to snicker when you say sca redy **cat**), it doesn't negate their natural instinct of fidelity. Dogs have a long history of symbiotic and heroic relationships with people (not so much with cats). In fact, the American Humane Association sponsors the annual Hero Dog Awards, and there are many entries every year. One myth about dogs worth debunking is that they only see in black and white. Dogs do see colors, although not as vividly as we do. What they perceive we might describe as muted hues. They have far fewer color receptors, cones, on the retinas of their eyes than we do. As dogs always say, "Dogs rule; cats drool". (Dogs think cats get that saying backwards.) The collective noun for a motley <u>pack</u> of mongrel dogs, or curs, is a <u>cowardice</u>. But they're not the best example of man's best friend.

I could never quite understand how
We could get chocolate milk from a cow.
But I figured it out.
(Though I do have a doubt.)
I think it's from brown cows now.

What's the Scoop?

A dairy cow's super power is that it can produce about eight gallons of milk a day. If you don't think that's amazing, think about how heavy one gallon of milk is and then imagine trying to carry eight of them. All that milk is produced by an animal that only eats grass or fodder, which is very difficult to digest. Thus, it must go through a twofold process of breaking down for absorption by the body. Cows will eat till full, then regurgitate the contents of their stomach, chew the *cud*, and swallow it again to complete the digestion process. They spend about eight hours a day eating, eight hours chewing the cud, and eight hours sleeping. No wonder they produce eight gallons of milk. An Old English word for the plural of cow (and a default collective noun) is a <u>kine</u>. Chocolate milk is, of course, made by people. But a dairy cow eating cacao beans sounds like a good idea. Hum, I wonder.

To know me is to love me.

A rooster is quite the dandy.
To him every hen is eye candy.
He struts his stuff
Looking groomed and buff,
With a comb that's perpetually handy.

What's the Scoop?

The phrase "pecking order" originated with chickens. The rooster is at the top of the order, and the hens will peck at others lower than themselves in a rigid social structure. Hens may also peck at low ranking roosters, and thus we have the word "henpecked". There are about three times as many chickens in the world as there are people, far more than any other species of bird. It is impossible to get an accurate count, but there are probably over 22 billion of them since there are about 7.5 billion people. Maybe everything tastes like chicken because it is chicken. We eat more chicken than all other animals combined. Oddly enough, the first chickens in America immigrated with the Pilgrims. Oh, about the "comb", or cockscomb, that red fleshy growth on the tops of their heads obviously wouldn't work for combing hair. Its function, like the two wattles hanging down on the sides of their chins, is to regulate body temperature. Blood is cooled as it circulates through the comb and wattles, helping chickens avoid heat stroke on a hot day. This is similar to the reason why dogs pant, to cool the blood circulating through their tongues; but chickens' tongues are too small to work like that. A group of chickens is a <u>brood</u> or a <u>clutch</u>. They gather in cliques and gossip about who to peck on next.

My parrot thinks he can talk.
Whatever I say, he'll mock.
He'll jabber away
Throughout the day,
But every word sounds
like SQUAWK!

Somebody better listen to me!

What's the Scoop?

The persistent screeching behavior of parrots is only typical of caged birds. In the wild, most parrot shout outs get answered by another nearby bird. But without another bird around to shout back at them, pet parrots feel the necessity of longer and louder screeching to try to provoke a response. Parrots are the only birds that feed themselves with their feet. So, they literally and figuratively are always putting their feet in their mouths. A <u>flock</u> of them can be very entertaining. They constantly squawk and cavort, spinning around when they land or hanging upside down. That's why one collective noun for them is a word that means chaotic: <u>pandemonium</u>. However, that word was first used in John Milton's *Paradise Lost* as the name of the place for *all* (pan) *demons* (demonium). But parrots are much too fun-loving to be demons. How can you not love hearing, "Hello, pretty bird", over and over and over and over and over and over and...

Oh how I do enjoy
To annoy the Japanese koi.
I tease 'em, when I wish,
And call 'em goldfish.
Then they snub me and bubble, "Oh boy!"

What's the Scoop?

Koi fish are a species of carp that was selectively bred in Japan for coloration and temperament. They typically live about 25-30 years. But one pampered koi lived 226 years, and several others have exceeded 100. They can grow up to three feet long and can be trained to eat out of your hand. They are related to goldfish, but koi are well aware of their superior status over their diminutive kin. Try training a goldfish to do what a koi can do, and try keeping it alive that long too. If you think a koi is making eyes at you, it very well could be. The word *koi* literally means *passionate love*. An English equivalent might be a crush. This is another ironic twist on the meaning of words because a koi is a cold fish, and the expression *cold fish* means lacking emotion. Whoever named the koi should probably be given a do over. That person obviously didn't realize the fish named passionate love would only show appreciation by snubbing people and giving them the cold shoulder.

The strangest creature you'll ever see
Has got to be an anemone.
You'll say that can't
Not be a plant.
It looks like a bush or a tree.

What's the Scoop?

Sea anemones (pronounced a-NEM-o-nee) are animals. They are popular fish tank pets, similar to corals, sponges, and jellyfish. There are well over 1000 species in a wide variety of colors, sizes, and shapes. Many have stinging tentacles that paralyze fish so they can digest them. However, clownfish (think Nemo) are immune to the toxin and live in a symbiotic relationship with anemone. They clean their host and hide from predators in the tentacles, and occasionally read to them. There is no collective noun for anemones, which is odd because they are almost always found in groups. I couldn't think of anything. I'm stumped. Wait a minute, how about a <u>stump</u> of anemones. I'll bet you can do better than that. What can you come up with?

I meant a MOTORIZED Ferris wheel.

My rat won't play
on his wheel.
He says running
is no big deal.
But the kind
of a toy
He'd really enjoy
Is a mini
Ferris wheel.

What's the Scoop?

The rat is the first animal of the Chinese New Year cycle, and those born in the Year of the Rat are believed to display: ambition, cleanliness, creativity, intelligence, generosity, and compassion. Those attributes are the opposite of the popular Western perception of rats. But no wonder rats don't like running on a wheel going nowhere and accomplishing nothing. That's not who they are. There is a long list of collective nouns for rats. Although I usually select one that best fits the characterization of the animal, here is a list of several ways groups of rats have been labeled: <u>colony</u>, <u>horde</u>, <u>mischief</u>, <u>pack</u>, <u>plague</u>, and <u>swarm</u>. The word <u>plague</u> is on that list because fleas carrying the Bubonic Plague were spread by rats during the Middle Ages. It was called the Black Death and decimated most of the developed world at that time. Perhaps people should have been trying to figure out why the rats survived.

I love you, Farmer Brown.

Farmers should surely stop
Feeding pigs with only slop.
If pigs were fed
Ice cream instead,
They'd lick up every drop.

What's the Scoop?

Pigs are another frequently misunderstood animal. They are intelligent, clean, thrifty, and fastidious. They are not as messy as their reputation implies; they only roll around in mud to cool off. Like most domesticated animals, they use a designated toilet area away from their eating area. Smart. Pigs are the last animal in the Chinese New Year cycle. Not only do they display those admirable qualities, but they are associated with wealth. That's why we call any small container in which we save money a *piggy* bank—regardless of its shape.

And I don't have to wallow in mud to cool off.

Trained pigs were once prized by truffle hunters for their acute sense of smell. Truffles are expensive and rare edible mushrooms that grow on the roots of trees. However, pigs have lost that job to truffle dogs, who are more easily trained not to eat the valuable find. Apparently one trait pigs cannot overcome with training is their appetite. Not so smart.

Don't eat at an outdoor café
'Less the pigeons there look okay.
Whether they are well fed
Or appear nearly dead
Will tell you if you should stay.

What's the Scoop?

Pigeons are intelligent and sociable and have nearly always lived as domesticated birds. There is archeological evidence dating back 5000 years showing pigeons with people. Carrier pigeons, also called homing or messenger pigeons, were credited with saving thousands of lives during World Wars I and II in the twentieth century by delivering battlefield messages banded around their legs. Perhaps the most bizarre story of any bird is that of the passenger pigeon, once believed to be the most abundant bird in the world. Flocks of them were so dense they darkened the sky, and so loud their approach was mistaken for thunder. One observer in 1871 described the sound as 1000 threshing machines, 1000 steamboats, and 1000 railroad trains simultaneously passing. Because they were so tasty, the birds were harvested by commercial hunters who followed the flocks and used huge nets to catch them or smoke to asphyxiate them. Within about three decades, the size of flocks was reduced from hundreds of millions (some estimate billions) to dozens. Hunters were so thorough there were only a few pairs left in captivity by 1900. The last passenger pigeon died in 1914. It had gone from being the most abundant bird in the world to zero in a mere 50 years. The collective noun for pigeons is a <u>kit</u> or a <u>flight</u>. Pigeons have had a heroic and tragic history. So give a pigeon a handout when you can.

Wild Animals of the Americas

Her mouth says I'm happy, but the rest of her face says NOT!

Bats are most renown
For hanging around upside down.
They must be befuddled;
Their view is so muddled
A smile to them is a frown.

What's the Scoop?

The bat is the only flying **mammal*** (flying squirrels glide). Every other animal that can fly is either a bird or a bug (flying fish, frogs, and a few others also glide). Bats are not befuddled; our perception of them is muddled. Our fear of bats is probably the result of vampire stories. But only three species of bat, out of about a thousand, drink blood; and in such tiny amounts that it doesn't harm the host. Usually they feed on cattle that don't even know the bats are there. Another remarkable trait of bats is they "see" with their ears. Most of them have a sonar echolocation system. Flying at night, they send out high frequency sound waves, beyond our range of hearing, and can locate insects, either in flight or on the ground, by listening to the echoes of those waves. Bats fly at various angles around their target and thus can get a three-dimensional "image" of it using sound waves alone. Blind people have been known to train themselves to navigate their surroundings by listening to echoes like a bat. You can find a <u>colony</u> of bats hanging from the roofs of caves. Watch out for the slippery guano below.

You previously learned about **species in the footnote on June Bugs, also about **kingdom** and **phylum**, two of the top rankings in the classification of living organisms. The scientific system for the classification of life forms is called taxonomy. The third level in this seven-level ranking system is **class**. Mammals are one of five main classes of animals. The other classes are birds, fish, reptiles, and amphibians. Some important factors determining animal classes are: mammals have hair and the mothers produce milk, birds have feathers, fish have gills, reptiles have scales, and amphibians have gills when young and lungs when old. Those five classes of animals are all in the phylum vertebrate, having an internal skeleton. Remember that animals in the arthropod phylum have an exoskeleton. Their bodies are supported by an exterior structure rather than interior bones. About 85% of all animals are arthropods. This is an abbreviated explanation of scientific classification, but the seven levels are as follows: kingdom (animal or plant), phylum (vertebrate or invertebrate), class (mammal, bird, fish, reptile, or amphibian), order, family, genus, and species. The last four classifications vary by individual characteristics of the animal. You might be able to remember this by the mnemonic "<u>K</u>eep <u>p</u>lastic <u>c</u>overs <u>o</u>n or <u>f</u>ace <u>g</u>etting <u>s</u>limed". The first letter of each word is also the first letter of the categories of animal classification. On the next page are more visual memory aids.*

Kingdom
　　Phylum
　　　　Class
　　　　　　Order
　　　　　　　　Family
　　　　　　　　　　Genus
　　　　　　　　　　　　Species

K P C O F G S

Keep Plastic Cover On or Face Getting Slimed.

I love slime.

<u>K</u>angaroo <u>P</u>ig <u>C</u>heetah <u>O</u>strich <u>F</u>lamingo <u>G</u>oat <u>S</u>nail

We're on page **69**

Oooooooooo
sole mio.

A coyote's a filthy thing,
And its howling will always ring
For miles away.
To a coyote I'd say
The shower's the best place to sing.

What's the Scoop?

Coyotes (usually pronounced ky-O-tee) communicate with a broad range of vocal sounds: howls, yelps, cries, barks, growls, wails, and squeals. So three or four of them can make it sound like a twenty-piece ensemble. Imagine the acoustic reverberation of a <u>band</u> of coyotes singing *a cappella* in the shower. Do you remember another animal in this book whose collective noun was also a <u>band</u>? (Hint: It didn't sing, but it signed.) The coyote is a revered figure in many Native American legends. The stories vary among different tribes, but the coyote is always characterized as a crafty trickster, sometimes with the ability to assume human form. So the next time someone plays a dirty trick on you, think of them as a coyote in disguise. Dirty tricksters could always use a shower.

If a porcupine asks you to pet it,
Best tell him he better forget it.
And if you canoe,
It will want to come too;
But it'll chew your canoe, so don't let it.

What's the Scoop?

You'll probably never see a group of porcupines. But if on the off chance you do, you might want to know what to call it: a <u>prickle</u>. You'll be in a pickle if you ever meet a <u>prickle</u> of porcupines. Perhaps, if you show them you know their correct collective noun, they'll spare you. Each one has about 30,000 quills, and they never run out because they regrow lost ones. If you're wondering how they lose quills, think Ouch! They use them as defense against anyone who invades their personal space, and it works quite well. They can't throw their quills, but they can whip you with their tail or back into you. Quills are sharp and barbed and really hurt. They are made of the same material as your hair. We have about 150,000 hairs on our heads, but the thickness of our hair is roughly $1/1000^{th}$ that of a porcupine's quill. Like beavers, porcupines love to gnaw on tree bark. So watch where you park your wooden canoe in porcupine country. You could find yourself up a creek without a paddle—or a canoe.

You'll find a pot of gold
At the end of a rainbow, I'm told.
But where it runs out
On a rainbow trout,
A fish tail is all you'll behold.

What's the Scoop?

Fishermen have a reputation for exaggerating the size of their catch. Their hands get farther apart every time "I once caught a fish this big" gets retold. However, the fish tale in this limerick alludes to an old Irish legend that you'll find a pot of gold, guarded by a leprechaun at the end of a rainbow. Reaching the end of a rainbow is an impossible task because it is visible only when sunlight is refracted off water droplets in the air at a certain angle, like light waves refracted through a glass prism. When you see a rainbow in the misty spray of a waterfall, notice that the rainbow moves as you do. That's because the angle between you and the sun changes. So the lesson here is not to stress over trying to pursue phantom riches, but relax and enjoy one of the most therapeutic activities known to man—fishing. By the way, rainbow trout don't have much of a rainbow, just a reddish streak on their sides. One collective noun for trout is a <u>hover</u>. During spawning season, female trout will eject thousands of eggs; and the males will <u>hover</u> nearby ready to dart over and fertilize them. Another common noun for most fish, is a <u>shoal</u>; but people usually call it a <u>school</u>. You'd think that <u>school</u> would be more academically correct, but you'd be mistaken. A <u>school</u> of fish is one where they are lined up in neat rows, like students in school desks. A <u>shoal</u> is one where the fish are running amok, like some less academic classrooms.

Rattlesnakes have
a maraca,
And shake
it like they
want to rhumba.
But don't
take the chance
They want
you to dance.
Run away and yell,
"Ay, caramba!"

What's the Scoop?

Maracas, or rhumba shakers, are musical instruments, hollow gourds with dried beans inside that rattle when shaken. They keep rhythm for Latin dances such as the rhumba. Not coincidentally, a nest of rattlesnakes is called a rhumba, but it probably should be called a rumble. Rattlers have rings on their tails made of keratin (like your fingernails) with beads inside that rattle or buzz. They buzz when shaken really fast. That is not an invitation to dance; it's a warning to stay away. Rattlers are venomous pit vipers and can strike up to about two-thirds their body length. So a four-foot rattler could bite you from about 32 inches away. Each time rattlers shed their skins they add a new ring to their tail. Myth buster alert: It used to be thought you could tell the age of a rattlesnake by the number of rings on its tail. But young snakes can shed their skin more than once a year and old snakes may not grow enough in one year to shed at all. On that subject, we shed our skins about once a month. The outer layer of our skin flakes off like dust without our noticing. When a rattlesnake sticks out its tongue, it's not being obnoxious; it's smelling you. The tongue picks up particles in the air carrying odors. Then the snake passes its tongue over special sensors on the inside of its mouth. (No, just because it smells with its mouth and tongue doesn't mean it tastes with its nose) Also, rattlers, and other snakes, have a pit organ that functions like built-in night vision goggles. They can see warm-blooded animals at night by their infrared heat signature Most mammals are warm-blooded, generating their own body heat, but snakes are cold-blooded and depend on outside heat. The phrase *cold-blooded* has come to mean cruel or ruthless, but snakes are not like that. When it's cold, they're just cold.

Though nobody thinks that it's fair,
A bear never has to share.
For wherever it goes,
A bear always knows
That nobody wants to be there.

What's the Scoop?

The most common myth about bears worth debunking is that they hibernate. They don't. They have a long winter sleep, where they are relatively inactive through the cold winter months. But true hibernation means that the animal's heart rate and body temperature drop dramatically. A bear's body temperature comes down a little, like yours does when you sleep, but nowhere near enough to call it hibernation. Bears are loners. About the only time they gather in a group is when several share a den for the winter. So this is appropriately called a <u>sloth</u> of bears. Probably the reason they can't go into a state of hibernation is that they snore so loudly they keep waking each other up.

It clearly states in this law book the party of the first part shall turn the pages for the party of the second part.

The owl is quite well read.
It's the wisest of birds, it's been said.
It sees all points of view.
What an owl can do
Is turn eyes to the back of its head.

What's the Scoop?

Owls have two forward facing eyes, and thus the ability to focus both of them on one object. That produces binocular vision, the kind of vision we have. Most birds have eyes on each side of their head, and thus they see an object with only one eye at a time, monocular vision. The difference between binocular and monocular is like the difference between a 3D movie and a regular flat screen one. Owl eyeballs are pear shaped and much larger than ours, with about 5000 times the number of light sensitive receptors we have. However, those eyes are locked in their sockets and can't rotate; so the owl's field of vision is very narrow. This limitation is overcome because owls' necks have more vertebrates than ours, and they can rotate their heads about 280°. Our necks only rotate about 60°. An owl can also elevate its head much higher than we can and even turn its head upside down. That pretty well covers all points of view, kind of like a debate in the British <u>parliament</u>, the collective noun for owls. Owls apparently look stately and can hoot their opinion with a cultured British accent.

Chipmunks are cute, but they scurry.
They're always in such a big hurry.
Whenever I take
Their picture, they make
The picture to come out blurry.

What's the Scoop?

One collective noun for a group of chipmunks is a <u>scurry</u>. They are constantly foraging for food, which they carry in cheek pouches that can expand up to three times the size of their heads. That's why they never stop to say "cheese" for a photo op. They have been known to store up to 8 pounds of food for the winter, about 90 times their own body weight. They can't possibly eat it all, but that doesn't stop them from scurrying around for more. They store some food in their burrows and bury some in the ground. It's lucky for the environment they forget where they buried some of their stash. Some of the lost seeds will grow into plants and trees. Besides, if they ate everything they stowed away, they'd be too fat to scurry.

Alligators always look scrappy.
Even smiling, they never look happy.
But they still would be best
At a smiling contest,
'Cause their smiles always look so snappy.

What's the Scoop?

Large alligators can chomp down with almost 3000 pounds of force, more than any other animal on earth, including great white sharks. That's about one and a half tons of pressure—as much as the weight of a small car. Once they've clamped down, they can also spin around in a death roll, trying to tear off a bite. Alligators' mouths curve up at the corners and then down, resembling both a smile and a frown. This is because of their massive jaw muscles. Talk about snappy! Gators gather together in a <u>congregation</u>. If they seem particularly happy to greet you, I'd recommend moving to a different congregation—perhaps one with your own species.

If you spot a moose, take care. Don't stand too close and stare. A moose is so large If it starts to charge, A moose will spike your hair.

I'm going to spike more than your hair this time.

What's the Scoop?

Moose are the largest animals in the deer family. They can weight about 1200 pounds, stand over seven feet tall, and have antlers, called paddles, that can grow six feet wide and weigh about 40 pounds. There are more moose attacks each year than bear attacks. Most of them happen during calving season as a moose mother's protective instinct for her young is easily piqued. Usually people unknowingly provoke moose attacks by not taking proper precautions around them. Don't treat a moose—or any wild animal—like a pet. If you want to spike your hair, get some real hair mousse. A herd of moose can be called a <u>gang</u>. They get tattoos, wear baggy clothes, and hang out in bad neighborhoods looking for trouble.

Possums are slow, so instead of fleeing when in dire dread. They've a trick that's quite awesome. It's called playing possum. They faint straight away and play dead.

Wow! Looks really can kill.

What's the Scoop?

Possums, or opossums, look like humongous rats, but they're not rodents. They are the only mammals in the order marsupials living in North America. Most marsupials live in Australia, including kangaroos, wallabies, and koalas. All marsupials have a pouch for carrying their young, which are born underdeveloped and mature inside their mother's pouch. Possums are known for playing dead when threatened. This is an involuntary fainting response. Their tongue hangs out, their teeth are bared, and they emit a foul odor. They wake up after a while, hopefully when the predator is not focused on them, and waddle away to make their escape. Better to play dead than be dead. Also, possums have a real superpower. They are immune to most poisonous snake bites. A group is a whole passel o' possums. Passel is an Old English word. It's a variation of parcel, simply meaning a group. Perhaps passel has remained the favored collective noun because of alliterative coincidence. A parcel of possums is a passel of possums you might send in the mail.

I'm not mad. The whole world is. Everyone calls me a hare, and I'm bare.

Where is the hair on a hare?
There's not hardly any hair there.
Rabbits are furry,
But a hare's got to worry
That it hasn't a stitch to wear.

What's the Scoop?

The myth of hares being hairless is busted. First, they would more accurately be described as having fur, not hair. Although fur and hair are made of the same substance, an animal whose body is covered with thick hair is said to be *furry*. But the length of the fur on both the hare and the rabbit is about the same. Short haired hares, like jackrabbits (yes, they're not rabbits, but hares), live in hot climates, and long haired ones, like arctic hares, live in cold climates. To emphasize the point, collective nouns for hares can be either a <u>down</u> or a <u>husk</u>. Down, meaning soft and fluffy like fine bird feathers, describes long haired hares; and husk, meaning a coarse outer covering like an ear of corn, describes short haired hares. The most noticeable difference between rabbits and hares is that hares are larger and faster. They are able to bound at speeds of around 35 mph. However, in Aesop's fable (spoiler alert) Hare still loses to Slow and Steady, the tortoise. During mating season around the month of March, male hares box and jump straight up for no apparent reason, thus inspiring the expression "Mad as a March hare". Lewis Carroll popularized this characterization with the March Hare at the Hatter's tea party in *Alice's Adventures in Wonderland*. You might enjoy reading that book now that you're done reading this one. It's one of my favorites.

What Did You Scoop Up?

Why is there always so much stuff to pick up under this branch?

We're on page 81

I love to learn, but I hated tests when I was in school. However, I loved games. So these activities are games. Match each animal from the list on the left with its description on the right. Write the letter in the blank corresponding to the animal.

Zoo Animals & Exotic Creatures

What animal...

1. ____ Giraffe
2. ____ Chimpanzee
3. ____ Warthog
4. ____ Gorilla
5. ____ Elephant
6. ____ Gnu
7. ____ Cheetah
8. ____ Octopus
9. ____ Lion
10. ____ Koala
11. ____ Kangaroo
12. ____ Hippopotamus

A. secretes "blood sweat" that acts as a lotion and sunscreen for their skin?
B. can change the color and shape of its skin to match its surroundings?
C. can sleep up to 20 hours a day?
D. has ossicones on its head, but no one knows why?
E. has hard bumps on its snout that store fat, like a camel's hump?
F. migrates in a herd called an implausibility?
G. can jump up to 12 feet high and 40 feet long?
H. looks like a teddy bear, but it's not a bear?
I. communicates by thumping its chest?
J. can remember past friends and places for at least 30 years?
K. can grip with its feet as well as it can with its hands?
L. can accelerate from 0 to 60 in about 3 seconds?

Bugs, Spiders & Creeping Crawlers

What animal...

1. ____ Beetle
2. ____ Moth
3. ____ Centipede
4. ____ Fly
5. ____ Tarantula
6. ____ Worm
7. ____ Dragonfly
8. ____ Spider
9. ____ Ladybug
10. ____ Ant
11. ____ Snail
12. ____ Mosquito

A. can flick tiny barbed hairs from its underbelly to repel predators?
B. has about 400,000 different species?
C. is always venomous, except for one family but very few are harmful to people?
D. breathes through its skin?
E. has about 30,000 lenses in each eye and has 360° vision?
F. secretes a smelly obnoxious substance from its leg joints to repel predators?
G. travels about 50 yards per hour on a trail of slime?
H. is often accused of eating clothes yet many adults have no mouths?
I. is the deadliest animal in the world and the costliest to control?
J. can lift 100 times its own body weight?
K. vomits digestive juices on its food and then sucks it up?
L. has a name that means 100 legs, but none of them ever have exactly that many legs?

Birds from Around the World

What animal...

1. _____ Peregrine Falcon
2. _____ Raven
3. _____ Peacock
4. _____ Penguin
5. _____ Duck
6. _____ Toucan
7. _____ Eagle
8. _____ Vulture
9. _____ Stork
10. _____ Ostrich
11. _____ Woodpecker
12. _____ Flamingo

A. can spot small prey from high in the sky about two miles away?
B. is the largest and fastest running bird in the world?
C. has the largest bill compared to its body size?
D. only lives in the southern hemisphere?
E. is one of the smartest of all animal species and can mimic human speech?
F. eats by scraping its bill upside down through shallow muddy water?
G. flies in skein and times the flap of its wings with the updraft from the bird in front of it?
H. has a brain engulfed by gel to protect it from hard knocks?
I. can turn its head almost completely around and upside down?
J. can snap its bill shut to catch fish faster than almost any other animal?
K. has special features to protect its eyes and nostrils when it dives in a stoop?
L. has iridescent tail feathers with ocelli on them?

Domesticated Animals & Pets

What animal...

1. ____ Rabbit
2. ____ Cat
3. ____ Goat
4. ____ Dog
5. ____ Cow
6. ____ Chicken
7. ____ Parrot
8. ____ Koi
9. ____ Anemone
10. ____ Rat
11. ____ Pig
12. ____ Pigeon

A. can make a low rumbling sound considered therapeutic and conducive to healing?
B. can produce about eight gallons of milk every day?
C. is an ancient symbol of fertility?
D. achieved internet fame for having myotonia, fainting paralysis?
E. is the most populace bird in the world, with about three times as many as there are people?
F. has a name meaning "passionate love", but doesn't live up to it?
G. saved thousands of lives during both World Wars by carrying messages?
H. looks more like a plant than an animal?
I. spread Bubonic Plague throughout most of the world during the Middle Ages?
J. eats with its feet and often puts its foot in its mouth?
K. is honored at an annual awards ceremony for heroism and loyalty?
L. is believed to be thrifty and has a name used for money containers?

Wild Animals of the Americas

What animal...

1. ____ Bat
2. ____ Coyote
3. ____ Porcupine
4. ____ Rainbow Trout
5. ____ Rattlesnake
6. ____ Bear
7. ____ Owl
8. ____ Chipmunk
9. ____ Alligator
10. ____ Moose
11. ____ Possum
12. ____ Hare

A. chomps down with 1500 pounds of force?
B. is a trickster spirit in Native American lore?
C. is associated with March Madness (and isn't even a college basketball fan)?
D. smells with its tongue and mouth?
E. can weigh about 1200 pounds and has paddles?
F. can store up to 90 times its own body weight in food?
G. is the only marsupial in North America?
H. Is the only flying mammal?
I. gathers in a shoal, but it's usually called a school?
J. is said to hibernate, but really only has a winter sleep?
K. protects itself with about 30,000 sharp barbed quills?
L. can twist its head almost completely around and turn it upside down?

Classifying What You Scooped Up

The scientific classification of what you scooped up from this book is called taxonomy. In the section about taxonomy on pages 67–68, I mention that the presentation in this book is an abbreviated version of the complete scientific system. Taxonomists have added a couple other classifications above Kingdom to include life forms that are neither plant nor animal, such as fungus and bacteria. We are not going to focus on all the complex forms of life here, just on the classification of animals. I should also note there are some sub-categories for each ranking, such as the previously mentioned subspecies of domesticated dogs. Let's see if the memory aids helped you remember the classification rankings. Put the following list in the proper order by putting the number 1 for the highest ranking down to 7 for the lowest.

____ Class

____ Genus

____ Kingdom

____ Order

____ Species

____ Family

____ Phylum

Making Tracks After Stepping in the Footnotes

This game is for students ten and up. Did you get the information in the footnotes following the first entry in each chapter? Go back and reread the footnotes, then fill in the blanks with the correct word. It's okay to look up the answers. Some of these words are very challenging, even for ardent verbophiles. When you're done give yourself a high-5, or a high-10 if no one else is around; you deserve it.

1. Lovers of words are called _____. (Hint: Read the instructions).

2. The study of word origins is called _____.

3. There are about 1.4 million known species of life forms in the world, but scientists believe there may be approximately _____ million more yet to be discovered.

4. About _____ new species are discovered every year.

5. The gravitational force you feel on your body now is about _____. (Hint: this is a compound word).

6. Several extreme rollercoasters are rated around _____, the maximum amount of g force you will experience on the ride.

7. People are usually allergic to _____ that are on an animal's fur, not to the fur itself.

8. About _____ percent of pet owners are allergic to their pets, but choose to endure the symptoms for their love of the animal.

9. The scientific classification of life forms is called _____.

10. Only animals in the phylum _____ are included in the chapter *Bugs, Spiders, and Creeping Crawlers*.

We're on page **88**

Digging for the Source

Identify each animal below and put its first letter in the correspondingly numbered spaces on the next page. If you dig deeply you will find the source.

1. I can tap my beak 20 times per second to get food and communicate.
2. I sleep underwater and can come up for air without waking up.
3. I am a tiny insect whose total body mass worldwide adds up to about the same mass as the human population.
4. I can carry around my very large bill because it's mostly hollow.
5. I am an insect that is accused of eating clothes, even though I may not have a mouth as an adult.
6. I can chomp down with as much force as a small car.
7. I am a reptile that can see body heat, which helps me hunt at night.
8. I can detect methane gas from a mile away.
9. I have a long nose that can lift up to 600 pounds and smell 5000 times better than human noses.
10. My roar can be heard by others of my kind up to 30 miles away.
11. I travel slowly, but I make a smooth path to slide on wherever I go.
12. I have cooperatively dismantled poacher traps designed to catch me.
13. I have three hearts that pump blue blood.
14. I can fly better than any other animal with two sets of independently rotatable wings.
15. I am the fastest of all <u>small</u> land animals, and I'm not mad.
16. I only weigh a few ounces, but I can carry 100 times my own weight.
17. I can snap my bill shut in 25 milliseconds to catch fish.
18. I can walk upright on the ground, but prefer to swing from trees.
19. I am a bird ranked as one of the most intelligent of all animals.
20. I am a raptor with eyes that can spot small prey from two miles away.
21. I am an animal that looks like a plant and lives in the ocean.
22. I am the largest of all spiders, one of my kind can catch and eat rats, lizards, snakes, and birds.
23. I can remember old friends and past feeding places for at least 30 years.
24. I can migrate thousands of miles with a little help from the wind vortex of the bird in front of me.

We're on page **89**

___ ___ ___ ___   ___ ___ ___ ___ ___ ___ ___
 1   2   3   4   5   6   7   8   9 10 11

___ ___ ___   ___ ___ ___
12 13 14   15 16 17

___ ___ ___ ___ ___ ___ ___!
18 19 20 21 22 23 24

The more we discover about the mysteries of life on Earth, the more we must inevitably be drawn to discover the source of its creation.

Now I'm a right-hand bookend. I'm still not sure why. But I did have fun keeping track of the pages for you.

We all must long for the day
When we, like the animals, may
Find a purpose and place
That we can embrace;
So let's have fun on the way.

We're at **The End**.  I'm still a little confused though. How did all those animals get out on that limb, and where did they all go?

Answer Key:

Matching

Zoo	Bugs	Birds	Pets	Wild
1. D	1. B	1. K	1. C	1. H
2. K	2. H	2. E	2. A	2. B
3. E	3. L	3. L	3. D	3. K
4. I	4. K	4. D	4. K	4. I
5. J	5. A	5. G	5. B	5. D
6. F	6. D	6. C	6. E	6. J
7. L	7. E	7. A	7. J	7. L
8. B	8. C	8. I	8. F	8. F
9. C	9. F	9. J	9. H	9. A
10. H	10. J	10. B	10. I	10. E
11. G	11. G	11. H	11. L	11. G
12. A	12. I	12. F	12. G	12. C

Classification

<u>3</u> Class
<u>6</u> Genus
<u>1</u> Kingdom
<u>4</u> Order
<u>7</u> Species
<u>5</u> Family
<u>2</u> Phylum

Footnotes

1. verbophiles
2. etymology
3. nine (9)
4. 10,000
5. one g
6. 5 g's
7. proteins
8. 1/5 (20%)
9. taxonomy
10. invertebrate

Digging

You'll have to work to solve this puzzle, but I encourage you to find the solution on your own. If you complete it, email me at the address on my contact page at uniqueinkpress.com. I will send you a special certificate. Keep digging for the source.

www.ingramcontent.com/pod-product-compliance
Lightning Source LLC
Chambersburg PA
CBHW080447110426
42743CB00016B/3306